INVESTING FOR
SUCCESS

RETHINKING **HVAC PLANT ROOM**
EXPENDITURE AND DEMAND**ROI**

INVESTING FOR
SUCCESS

RETHINKING **HVAC PLANT ROOM** EXPENDITURE AND DEMAND**ROI**

VIKRAM BANSAL

Worldwide Published by
Pendown Press

PENDOWN PRESS LLP
An ISO 9001 & ISO 14001 Certified Co.,
Regd. Office: 3767A, Kanhaiya Nagar,
Tri Nagar, Delhi-110035
Ph.: 8180886000, 9650072927, 8595249536
E-mail: info@pendownpress.com
Branch Office: 1A/2A, 20, Hari Sadan, Ansari Road,
Daryaganj, New Delhi-110002
Ph.: 011-45794768
Website: PendownPress.com

First Edition: 2023

ISBN: 978-93-5554-931-0

All Rights Reserved
All the ideas and thoughts in this book are given by the 'author, and' he is responsible for the treatise,' facts, and' dialogues used in this book. He is also responsible for the 'pictures used' and the permission to use them in this book. Copyright of this book is reserved with the author. The publisher does not have any responsibility for the above-mentioned matters. No part of this publication may be reproduced, distributed, or transmitted in any form or by any means, including photocopying, recording, or other electronic or mechanical methods, without the prior written permission of the publisher and author.

Layout Designed by Pendown Graphics Team
Cover Designed : www.absolutefactor.com
Photo Courtesy : Md Zarandah
Printed and Bound in India by Thomson Press India Ltd.

Contents

Preface

Investing time, effort, and resources in our professional development not only yields significant returns but also offers a sense of fulfilment that surpasses any other investment we may undertake. Enhancing one's quality of life entails the pursuit of effectiveness and success in many endeavours, ultimately enabling individuals to experience personal fulfilment and satisfaction. Investing in both personal and professional growth has a significant impact on the overall quality of an individual's life, both in the present and the future. This book serves as a valuable resource for professionals in the HVAC sector who aspire to transform their business practises and advance the cause of energy conservation. I have made extensive efforts to ensure comprehensive dissemination of knowledge to my readers.

Many people have found themselves in situations where they felt that a project was unproductive and lacked viable solutions. Subsequently, individuals inside our social circles, including classmates, friends, mentors, or individuals with more experience, may present a straightforward approach that had not previously been considered by us. By what means did they arrive at the solution in such a prompt manner?

While it is possible that they possess sufficient expertise, it is worth considering the possibility that the solution they have discovered is really commonplace and easily attainable with minimal effort. The objective of this book is to provide knowledge and enhance the capabilities of building owners, CFOs, CXOs, facilities managers, and chief engineers when it comes to understanding the economic and ecological benefits of prioritising HVAC efficiency. My objective is to effectuate a shift in the approach to HVAC investments in commercial buildings by sharing my expertise, personal experiences, and practical methodologies. Given the upcoming developments, the necessity to reconsider energy consumption is imperative in light of future developments. It is expected that this literary work will serve as a catalyst for the aforementioned transformation.

This book endeavours to empower readers by imparting my personal experiences and the valuable lessons I have learned. Its goal is to enable readers to make well-informed judgements that transcend mere immediate cost considerations. On the contrary, it promotes the prioritisation of the long-term advantages associated with optimising HVAC systems to achieve optimal efficiency and return on investment. Collectively, it is possible to cultivate a more promising future characterised by the fundamental principles of energy efficiency, exceptional performance, and enduring sustainability, which serve as the cornerstones of achievement.

About the Author

Energy Optimisation Expert, Vikram Bansal has over 17 years of impressive industry experience. He has progressed up the ladder in the field of managing reasonably prestigious project of well- known brands in the area of HVAC & IAQ. He has honed the skills necessary to conduct precise energy audits within his area of expertise.

Beyond his technical prowess, Vikram is recognized as an IAQ Improvement Expert and a devoted team builder who is always willing to work according to the requirements. He enjoys taking responsibility for his task with a positive attitude. He seeks a challenging position in the HVAC industry which demands innovation, creativity, and dedication. Such a role would enable him to continue working in a demanding and fast-paced environment, utilising current knowledge and nurturing creativity while providing ample opportunities for learning.

In 2011, he formed his company, Nirvay Solutions with a mission to create a team of competent people to 'add efficiency to energy requirement with appropriate technology'. With a prime focus to offer the state-of-art products and services to its clients, the company has successfully executed over 500 projects, consistently reducing their operational energy costs for their clientele.

Acknowledgement

I want to express my gratitude to all the individuals who have supported me throughout my life because without them, I would not be who I am. I would like to acknowledge and extend my gratitude to those people who have played a pivotal role in the success of this book.

First and foremost, I would want to express my sincere gratitude to my parents for always being the source of comfort for me during difficult times. They instilled in me the discipline and values that have been instrumental in my life's journey.

My wife, Rashi, and my children's tremendous kindness and concern have motivated me to write every day. I appreciate your support.

A special thanks to my mentors, Akshar Yadav and Suresh Mansharamani, who inspired me to write this book and had a big influence on my life.

I will always be grateful to Mukesh Pandey and Prashant Kabra for being supportive in my entrepreneur journey.

And I can't forget to thank my colleagues and team at Nirvay Solutions (P) Limited. This book wouldn't exist without your help and experiences. Thank you for everything.

Chapter 1

A Journey Shaped by Problem-Solving Mentality

Early Influences and Upbringing

Growing up in a small village in Punjab, I was immersed in a business-oriented family. However, my father took a different path and pursued a job in the Reserve Bank of India. He instilled in me the values of hard work, self-reliance, and problem-solving. Our modest means taught me the importance of making the most of what we had and finding innovative solutions to challenges.

Developing a Passion for Numbers

Among my father's exceptional qualities was his ability to solve complex problems without relying on calculators or technology. He imparted to me the skills of number manipulation and accurate calculations. This early exposure to numerical analysis sparked my love for mathematics and its practical applications. I came to realize that numbers hold the power to unlock solutions and drive decision-making.

The Scooter Challenge and the Birth of Problem-Solving Skills

On my 18th birthday, I expressed my wish for a scooter to aid in my studies to my father. Instead of fulfilling my request outright, he threw a challenge my way. He asked me to plan a family function and execute it within a budget 20% lower than the original estimate. If I succeeded, he would reward me with the scooter. This challenge put my problem-solving skills to the ultimate test.

Driven by my passion for numbers and my determination to overcome any obstacle, I meticulously planned the function, finding ways to reduce costs without compromising on the comfort of our guests or the essence of the event. Through resourcefulness and collaboration with my friends, I managed to achieve an impressive 25% cost savings. The successful execution of the function earned me not only the scooter but also the reputation of being someone who never gives up, no matter the challenges faced.

Chapter 2

From Engineer
to Entrepreneur

Joining Voltas Limited: Saving Energy and Gaining Recognition

With a degree in Mechanical Engineering in hand, I embarked on an exciting professional journey. The opportunity to join Voltas Limited, a renowned company in the HVAC industry and a subsidiary of the esteemed Tata Group, was a dream come true. My role as a sales engineer, my primary goal was to collaborate with designers and building owners, working towards optimizing air conditioning loads while enhancing indoor air quality.

During my tenure at Voltas, I worked closely with prominent consultants and played a pivotal role in saving approximately 5,000 TR of energy across multiple projects. These impactful energy-saving initiatives showcased an impressive average return on investment (ROI) of less than three years. Recognizing my achievements and exceptional problem-solving abilities, I was selected as one of the top ten potential managers among 200 employees at Voltas, globally.

Fueled by Entrepreneurial Aspirations

Despite achieving success and recognition at Voltas, I felt a growing desire to make an even greater impact in the energy sector. The vibrant culture at the Tata Group, combined with the guidance and support of my mentor, Ashwani Sharma, fueled my entrepreneurial aspirations. In 2011, driven by sheer determination, I took a leap of faith and founded Nirvay Solutions, a company dedicated to saving energy through effective management of air and water flow in HVAC systems.

Founding Nirvay Solutions: A Mission to Save Energy

Nirvay Solutions was not without its difficulties. I lacked prior experience and specific business skills as a first-time entrepreneur. Nevertheless, with unwavering determination and the support of consultants and colleagues who believed in my vision, I embarked on a mission to revolutionize the HVAC industry and promote energy conservation.

As time passed, Nirvay Solutions began to create a significant impact through fruitful collaborations with esteemed organisations such as ABB and Armstrong. Additionally, our active participation in notable projects such as the Lucknow Secretariat, Lucknow High Court, Kailash Hospitals, OP Jindal University, and Chandigarh University further solidified our presence in the market. Recognizing our remarkable contributions, Global Hues honored us with the esteemed Best CEO award in 2022. Moreover, our emphasis on energy savings has resulted in more than INR 100 crore in savings for our valued clients.

Projects of Note and Collaboration with Industry Leaders

Working with industry leaders and undertaking prestigious projects opened up new opportunities for Nirvay Solutions. Our ability to demonstrate the effectiveness of our energy-saving strategies in a variety of settings, including hospitals, IT/ITES buildings, shopping malls, and hotels, highlighted the importance of ROI and the important role played by HVAC systems in overall energy efficiency.

As our reputation grew, we began to attract the attention of major industry stakeholders. The positive results obtained as a result of our implementation of advanced technologies and optimised designs cemented our position as an industry leader. With every project, we continuously refined our approach, developed new strategies, and fine-tuned our commitment to prioritised long-term returns over immediate expenses.

Chapter 3

The Goal of This Book

The Unknown Fact About HVAC Systems

Over the past 5 years, I have gained valuable experience working with a client who was passionate about increasing energy efficiency and reducing HVAC costs in his building. This was a pivotal moment for me, as I realized the growing need to conserve energy and make buildings more sustainable for the sake of our planet. With energy prices on the rise, ROI and efficiency must take priority over upfront costs. This has become my calling — to contribute to sustainability through energy conservation. My business gives me the opportunity to make a real impact, aligning with my personal passion. I have set an ambitious goal to save 1 crore kWh over the next 5 years across my client base. The purpose of this book is to educate and empower building owners, CFOs, CXOs, facilities managers, and chief engineers about the financial and environmental benefits of focusing on HVAC efficiency. By sharing my knowledge, experiences, and practical strategies, I aim to drive change in how commercial buildings approach HVAC investments. The future demands that we rethink energy usage. I hope this book will be a catalyst for that change.

ROI - The North Star for HVAC Guidance

It pains me to see consultants and building owners adrift at sea following short-sighted HVAC decisions. Errors in these crucial equipment selections lead to a downstream cascade of wasted time, money, and effort as they attempt to rectify their course.

Much like sailors navigating without a compass, they lose sight of the ultimate destination - long-term efficiency and cost savings. In the fog of upfront purchase prices, the guiding light of ROI fades from view. Only later does the harsh reality set in, when the inadequate equipment fails to deliver projected performance.

I have witnessed this unfortunate journey stray off course far too often. Out of these storms of mismanagement, my passion was born to be a ROI lighthouse, illuminating the path to secure decisions. This book provides the navigation tools to avoid the rocky shoals of equipment misjudgments.

ROI analysis will serve as your Polaris, ensuring your objectives remain aligned and your investments are safeguarded. My mission is to empower well-informed choices that withstand challenges, both anticipated and unforeseen. Together, we will correct the course and navigate towards a horizon of optimization, energy conservation, and sustainability for years to come. Your HVAC journey commences here.

Unlocking a Brighter Future: Sustainable Practices and Energy Efficiency

It is clear that every project is unique and must be treated as such. The focus should be on designing for optimal ROI, considering the specific requirements of each project. Research has proven that well-designed and properly executed projects are over 30% more efficient and 40% more cost-effective over their life cycles compared to poorly executed ones. Embracing sustainable practices and giving priority to energy efficiency open the doors to a brighter and more sustainable future.

By sharing my experiences and lessons learned, this book aims to empower readers to make informed decisions that go beyond immediate cost considerations. Instead, it encourages prioritizing the long-term benefits of optimising HVAC systems for maximum efficiency and ROI. Together, we can create a brighter future where energy efficiency, top-notch performance, and long-term viability are the pillars of success.

Chapter 4

Case Study: The University Project

District Cooling and the Challenge of Air Conditioning Ten Hostel Towers

One notable project that exemplifies the importance of prioritising ROI and optimising HVAC systems is the University project. The project involved the centralised air conditioning of ten hostel towers, with construction staggered over time. The farthest tower was situated over a kilometer away from the plant room, making it a perfect case for district cooling.

Proposing the Primary Variable and Tertiary Variable Systems

To eliminate the complexities of piping running to the towers, we proposed the use of a primary variable and tertiary variable system. This cutting-edge solution allowed us to account for the variable air conditioning load of individual towers and ensure optimal energy efficiency. By conducting a thorough analysis of the maximum heat required and utilizing intelligent control systems, we could adjust the speed of the pumps and save energy during periods of low demand. This innovative strategy also eliminated the need for a complex secondary pumping system, simplifying the overall design.

Overcoming Resistance: The Value of VFDs in Pumps

Introducing Variable Frequency Drives (VFDs) in the pumps was a significant expense that the designer and client initially hesitated to accept. However, I was quick to identify the long-term benefits and potential ROI of this investment. After conducting a thorough analysis, calculating the payback period and demonstrating the energy savings that could be achieved. With an attractive ROI of less than two years, the client understood that this investment was not an expense but, in fact, rather a smart decision that would yield long-term financial benefits.

4.4 Calculating ROI and Conveying the Value of Investment

To reinforce the value of the investment in VFDs, I presented the client with a detailed ROI analysis. By highlighting the substantial energy savings, reduced operational costs, and improved efficiency, I effectively communicated how this investment would contribute to the overall profitability of the project. With a clear understanding of the long-term advantages, the client agreed to proceed with the VFDs, recognizing it as a strategic investment rather than an additional expense.

Primary Chilled Water Pump Savings			
Site Location	Sonipat		
Description	Conventional End suction	Our Proposed Pump	Remarks
Application	Primary Pump	Primary Pump	
Pump Type	End suction	Vertical In line with VFD mounted (sensor less technology)	
Total No. of Pumps	1	1	
Design Flow in GPM	1440	1440	
Design Head in mtr	65	65	
Motor Rating in KW	90.0	90.0	
No. of Working Pump	1	1	
Inbuilt Flow Meter	Not Available	Available	
IoT Enabled	No	Yes	Mechanical equipment with cloud-based analytics and digital controls perfectly integrated for reliability and efficiency.
Integrated VFD	Not Available	Yes	Motor Mounted with an inbuilt VFD, equipped with a flow meter and digital display to view all critical parameters of the pump, such as Flow, Head, Power, and RPM.

RPM	2985	1667	
Pump Efficiency	78	80	
Annual Operating Hour (HRS)	3240	3240	Considering 9 months operation for 12 hours per day.
Ikw of one Pump at 100% Load	74.53	72.32	
KW consumption	74.53	61.47	(Considering 15% less due to various safety factors in head calculation).
Total Load consumption in a year (KWH)	241477	199169	
Rate per kwh	10.0	10.0	
Total operating cost in Rs.	2414772	1991693	
Operating Cost Saving per year in Rs	423079		
Capital Cost	800000	1570000	
ROI in years	3.7		To recover the entire capital cost of the pump.
ROI in years	1.8		To recover the differential cost of the pump.

Chapter 5

Pitfalls & Lessons Learned

Deviations and Unforeseen Consequences

Despite our best efforts, sometimes deviations from the agreed-upon design can sometimes occur during the procurement stage. Such deviations can have significant consequences for the performance and energy efficiency of the HVAC system. In the University project, for instance, the HVAC contractor requested the removal of VFDs and proposed using normal VFDs instead, leading to unforeseen challenges and suboptimal results.

Recognizing the Importance of Following Design Specifications

It became clear that the contractor did not fully grasp the essence of the project and the significance of adhering to the original design. This led to power losses, discomfort for occupants, and a departure from the anticipated ROI. Reflecting on this experience, I realized the importance of assertively communicating and reinforcing the value of design specifications to all stakeholders involved.

Analyzing Discomfort and Mitigating Negative Effects

When the client expressed dissatisfaction with the air conditioning's comfort and the inability to achieve the anticipated ROI, immediate action was taken. Working closely with my team, we conducted a comprehensive analysis of the system, spending five days meticulously investigating the issues. Our examination revealed that several factors contributing to the discomfort and energy inefficiency were linked to deviations made during the procurement stage.

To rectify the situation to the best of our abilities, we implemented the necessary steps, mitigating the negative effects and enhancing system functionality. Recognizing the significance of proper operation, we understood the importance of running the equipment in auto mode rather than manual mode. We organised special training sessions on-site to educate the operators about the correct procedures and the energy-saving potential of the system.

The Next Phase: Embracing the Original Design and Achieving ROI

Armed with valuable lessons learned from the challenges faced in the University project, we embarked on the next phase with renewed determination to adhere strictly to the original design specifications. The client understood the importance of the initial design and the value it brought in terms of energy efficiency and ROI. As a result, the intended design was implemented without any deviations in the following phase.

The ROI for the second phase pleasantly surprised us, with a remarkable payback period of less than 14 months and an impressive return on investment of 200% within three years. This success reaffirmed the importance of prioritizing design integrity and sticking to the original plan, reinforcing the notion that treating the plant room as an investment, rather than an expense, leads to significant financial benefits.

Primary Chilled Water Pump Savings			
Site Location		Sonipat	
Description	Conventional End suction	Our Proposed Pump	Remarks
Application	Primary Pump	Primary Pump	
Pump Type	End suction	Vertical In line with VFD mounted (sensor less technology)	
Total No. of Pumps	1	1	
Desing Flow in GPM	1440	1440	
Design Head in mtr	65	65	
Motor Rating in KW	90.0	90	
No. of Working Pump	1	1	
Inbuilt Flow Meter	Not Available	Available	

IoT Enabled	No	Yes	Mechanical equipment with cloud-based analytics and digital controls is perfectly integrated for reliability and efficiency.
Integrated VFD	Not Available	Yes	The motor is mounted with an inbuilt VFD and equipped with a flow meter and a digital display to view all critical parameters of the pump, such as Flow, Head, Power, and RPM.
RPM	2985	1667	
Pump Efficiency	78	79.97	
Annual Operating Hour (HRS)	3240	3240	Considering 9 months operation for 12 hours per day.
Ikw of one Pump at 100% Load	74.53	72.32	
KW consumption	74.53	61.47	43.80 The actual head is less than the design head, as the full project and farthest building have not yet been completed at this time. It took 3 years for the actual farthest hostel to be constructed.

Total Load consumption in a year (KWH)	241477	199169	141912	
Rate per kwh	10.0	10.0	10.0	
Total operating cost in Rs.	2414772	1991693	1419120	
Actual Operating Cost Saving per year in Rs	995652			
Capital Cost (year 2016)	800000	1570000	1570000	
Actual ROI in years	1.6			To recover the entire capital cost of the pump.
Actual ROI in years	0.8			To recover the differential cost of the pump.

Chapter 6

The Effectiveness of Equipment Synchronisation

Recognizing the Relationship Between Variable Pumping Systems and Chiller Loads

A common inefficiency often observed in many plant rooms is the imbalance between the variable pumping system, running at 100% load, and chillers, operating at only 70% load. This mismatch results in excessive power consumption and higher energy costs. To optimize energy usage and achieve maximum efficiency, it is critical to understand the relationship between the variable pumping system and chiller loads.

Addressing Issues and Increasing Energy Savings

To effectively tackle this issue, several critical aspects demand attention. Firstly, it is essential to ensure that variable systems (chillers, pumps, AHU, valves) operate in auto mode rather than manual mode. This allows the system to synchronise with the changing load of the building and optimizing the energy consumption accordingly.

Furthermore, performing proper heat exchange analysis at the air handling unit (AHU) coil level can assist in identifying and correcting inefficiencies that may contribute to unnecessary chilled water consumption.

Smart VFDs and Remote Monitoring Play a Role

The HVAC industry is witnessing a revolutionary change, with technological advancements, particularly the integration of Artificial Intelligence (AI) and Machine Learning (ML). AI-enabled smart VFDs can not only monitor the system's performance but also generate detailed analyses and provide preventive maintenance notifications. Concurrently, remote monitoring tools have opened up a world of possibilities, allowing stakeholders to access real-time data from anywhere in the world. This seamless synergy of cutting-edge innovations has resulted in remarkable energy savings and heightened operational efficiency in the HVAC realm.

The Importance of Proper Balancing and Accessories

Proper balancing of accessories, such as two-way valves or PID valves, is critical to ensuring the system's efficiency. These elements play a crucial role in maintaining optimal flow rates and temperature control. To avoid energy losses and maintain peak performance, these accessories must undergo regular servicing and calibration.

Air Balancing and Duct Leakage: Regularly conduct air balancing to ensure proper airflow distribution throughout the building. Promptly address any duct leakage issues, as leaking air leads to wasted energy and reduced system efficiency. Sealing ductwork and maintaining proper insulation will minimize energy losses.

Building Envelope: Pay close attention to the building envelope by sealing air leaks, adding insulation, and optimizing glazing systems. A well-insulated and properly sealed building envelope helps reduce heating and cooling loads, resulting in energy savings.

Retro commissioning and Energy Audits

Conduct periodic retro commissioning and energy audits to identify system inefficiencies, fine-tune controls, and implement energy-saving measures.

Continuous Monitoring and Analysis

Utilize energy management systems to monitor HVAC equipment performance and energy consumption in real-time.

Analyse data trends to identify opportunities for optimization, detect anomalies, and proactively address issues.

Chapter 7

AI and Machine Learning are Transforming HVAC

Monitoring and Analyzing Plant Rooms with AI and ML

Traditionally, monitoring and analysing plant rooms in their entirety has been a challenging task for engineering teams due to the lack of efficient remote monitoring and analysis tools. However, with the emergence of AI and ML technologies, comprehensive solutions are now available. These tools can monitor and analyze the entire HVAC system, providing valuable insights into energy consumption patterns, identifying potential inefficiencies, and enabling proactive maintenance.

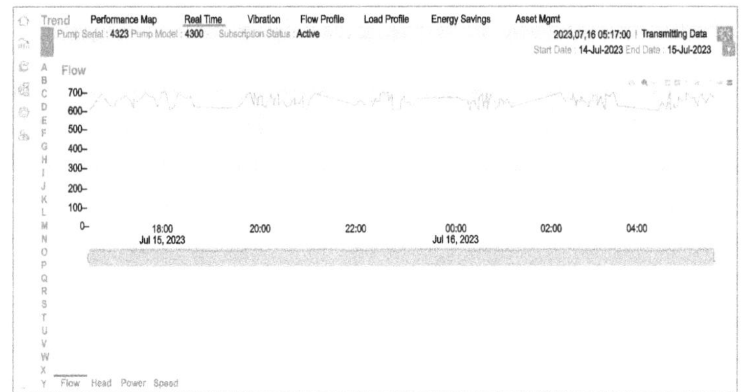

Fig.7.1: Pump actual performance

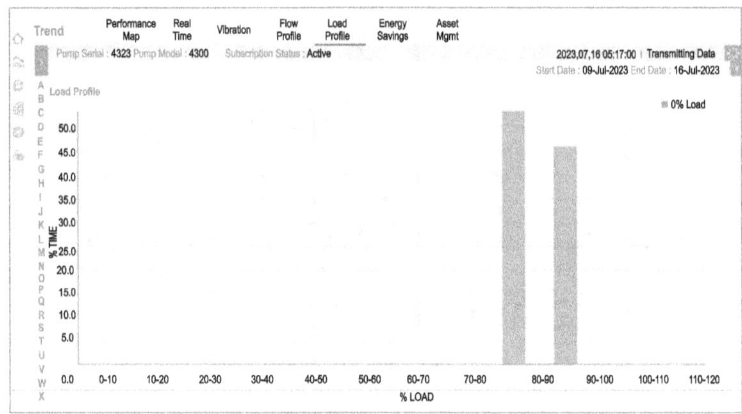

Fig.7.2: AI and ML decoding the actual Building Load profile

Enhancing Energy Savings and Preventive Maintenance

The utilization of AI and ML-powered tools empowers the generation of real-time data analysis, identifying energy-saving opportunities and areas for improvement. By leveraging these insights, stakeholders can implement targeted measures to optimize energy usage, reduce operational costs, and extend equipment lifespan. Additionally, these cutting-edge tools proactively detect maintenance issues, notifying stakeholders of potential problems and enabling preventive maintenance actions to minimize downtime and maximize system's overall efficiency.

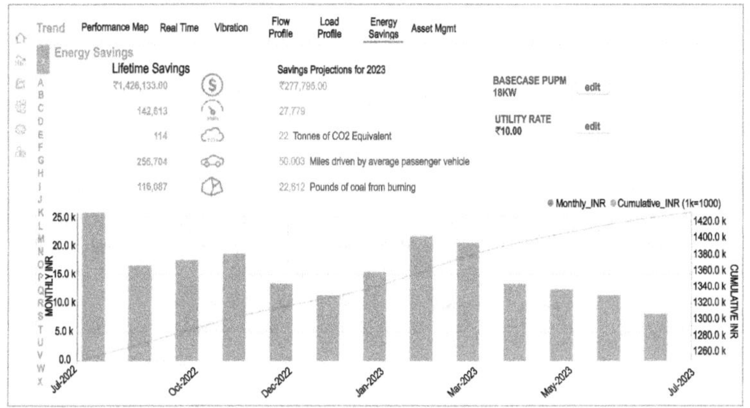

Fig.7.3: Energy savings mapping and recording

The Need for Clear SOPs and Remote Accessibility

To fully harness the benefits of AI and ML technologies, it is essential to establish clear Standard Operating Procedures (SOPs) for plant room operations. These SOPs serve as a guide, defining the best practices for utilizing the remote monitoring and analysis tools, enabling operators to master this advanced technology. With the introduction of remote connectivity to the monitoring system, stakeholders gain unrestricted access to vital information, real-time alerts, and data-driven decisions-making capabilities from anywhere, ensuring continuous optimization of the HVAC system.

Chapter 8

Every Project is Unique: Prioritizing ROI

Considering Specific Requirements for Optimal ROI

Each HVAC project is unique, and it is crucial to approach it with a thorough understanding of its specific requirements. Designing for optimal ROI involves considering factors such as building usage, occupancy patterns, climate conditions, and energy efficiency goals. By tailoring the HVAC system to meet these specific needs, stakeholders can achieve maximum energy savings and financial returns.

The Importance of Life Cycle Cost Analysis

To determine the true cost-effectiveness of an HVAC system, it is essential to conduct a comprehensive Life Cycle Cost (LCC) analysis. This analysis considers not only the upfront costs of equipment and installation but also factors in operational and maintenance expenses over the system's entire life cycle. By taking into account energy consumption, maintenance requirements, and equipment lifespan, stakeholders can make informed decisions that prioritize long-term savings and ROI.

Collaborative Decision-Making and Consultation

Effective decision-making requires collaboration and consultation among all stakeholders involved in the project. Engineers, designers, consultants, and building owners must work together to understand the project's goals, constraints, and budget. By fostering open communication and a shared understanding of the importance of ROI, stakeholders can collaboratively make well-considered choices that align with the project's financial objectives while also ensuring optimal performance and energy efficiency.

Value of Design Integrity

As industry professionals, it is our responsibility to emphasize on the importance of design integrity and the long-term benefits it brings. One may initially prioritise upfront cost savings, but by explaining and understanding the potential consequences of compromising on design and emphasising the value of optimised HVAC systems, we can shift the focus towards achieving long-term financial gains. Educating clients on the link between design decisions, energy efficiency, and ROI is paramount in fostering a shared commitment to lasting prosperity.

Chapter 9

The Future of Energy Efficiency

The Role of Renewable Energy and Green Technologies

The future of energy efficiency is undergoing a remarkable transformation as we embrace renewable energy sources and embrace the potential of green technologies. In the realm of HVAC systems, advancements in solar energy, geothermal systems, and energy storage solutions are leading the charge. By integrating these sustainable practices into HVAC system design, we can significantly reduce reliance on conventional energy sources and further enhance energy efficiency.

Embracing Smart Building Automation Systems

Energy efficiency finds new strength through the adoption of Smart Building Automation Systems (BAS). Embracing AI, ML, and Internet of Things (IoT) technologies, BAS has become the cornerstone of monitoring, controlling, and automating a wide array of building systems, including HVAC. By collecting real-time data, analyzing patterns, and adjusting settings based on occupancy and usage, BAS can achieve substantial energy savings and improve overall building performance.

Government Regulations and Incentives for Energy Efficiency

Government regulations and incentives are essential drivers of energy efficiency in the HVAC industry. As governments worldwide focus on sustainability and carbon reduction goals, they are implementing stricter regulations and offering financial incentives to encourage energy-efficient practices. By staying informed and taking advantage of these initiatives, stakeholders can align their projects with sustainability objectives while also reaping the benefits of reduced operational costs.

Continuous Improvement and Adaptation

The HVAC industry is constantly changing, with new technologies and strategies emerging on a regular basis. With new technologies and strategies emerging constantly, professionals must embrace change to stay relevant. Keeping a keen eye on industry trends, actively participating in conferences, seminars, and knowledge-sharing forums, we cultivate a culture of innovation that drives positive transformation. As we evolve towards efficiency, we shape a sustainable future for the HVAC sector, marked by progress and a commitment to environmental responsibility.

Epilogue

The journey from an engineer to an entrepreneur in the HVAC industry has been a remarkable one, filled with challenges, triumphs, and invaluable lessons. Throughout this book, we have explored the concept of viewing the HVAC plant room as an investment rather than an expense, as well as the importance of prioritizing ROI. We have delved into real-life stories, experiences, and strategies that illustrate how embracing the latest technology and design principles can result in significant financial gains and energy savings.

But our journey does not end here. The HVAC industry is constantly evolving, and new innovations and opportunities for improvement continue to arise. It is up to us, as industry professionals, to stay informed, adapt to emerging trends, and continually seek ways to optimize energy efficiency in our projects.

As you reach the end of this book, I urge you to take a moment and reflect on the valuable insights and knowledge you have gained. Now, consider how you can apply these principles and strategies into action in your own projects to create a positive impact on your clients, the environment, and your bottom line. Remember that every decision you make, whether it's about equipment selection or operational practices, plays a crucial role in enhancing the overall efficiency and sustainability of the HVAC system.

To stay at the forefront of industry advancements, remain connected and engaged. Attend conferences, participate in continuous learning, and keep yourself updated on the latest trends. Embrace new technologies such as AI, ML, and smart automation systems that have the potential to revolutionize energy efficiency in the HVAC industry. Collaborate with like-minded professionals, share best practices, and inspire others to prioritize long-term ROI in their projects.

By adopting a mindset of investment rather than expense, we can transform the perception of the HVAC plant room and drive significant financial benefits for our clients. We can create buildings that not only provide comfort and productivity but also minimize energy consumption and reduce environmental impact. Together, we can shape a future where sustainable practices and energy efficiency are at the core of every HVAC project.

Thank you for joining me on this journey. I encourage you to take the knowledge you've gained and transform it into action. Together, let us be catalysts for change and pioneers of energy-efficient HVAC systems. Let us build a future where the HVAC plant room is seen as an invaluable investment that brings both financial returns and a sustainable future.

Before we conclude this book, I would like to express my heartfelt gratitude to all those who have supported me throughout my journey in the HVAC industry. First and foremost, my deepest thanks go to my father, whose teachings of hard work, problem-solving, and resilience. His guidance and unwavering support have been instrumental in shaping my career.

I am also indebted to my mentors and colleagues at Voltas Limited, who have believed in my potential and provided me with valuable opportunities to grow and excel. Their guidance, expertise, and unwavering encouragement have been a cornerstone of my success.

I want to extend my thanks to the clients and consultants who have trusted me and allowed me to be a part of their projects. Your collaboration and belief in my vision have been the driving force behind my pursuit of excellence, spurring me on to deliver the best possible solutions.

I would also like to express my gratitude to the entire team at Nirvay Solutions for their hard work, dedication, and unwavering commitment to energy efficiency. Your passion and expertise have been the driving force behind our success.

Lastly, I want to thank my family and my mentor for their unwavering support, understanding, and encouragement. Your love and belief in me have been a constant source of motivation.

NOTES:

NOTES:

www.ingramcontent.com/pod-product-compliance
Lightning Source LLC
LaVergne TN
LVHW051313200726
843510LV00010B/1397